Unless otherwise indicated, all Scripture quotations are taken from the King James Version of the Bible.

I'M SOME IMPORTANT SHOES FOR THOSE PRETTY FEET

ISBN-13: 978-0692514283

Copyright © 2015 by Donte' L. Moore

Published by D. L. Moore and Associates LLC

49081 Whiskey Ln.

Tickfaw, LA 70466

Dedication

I would like to dedicate this book to my loving wife and beautiful family for being my biggest supporters and fans. To my beautiful wife Micah L. Moore who gives me the liberty to serve in the kingdom and is my strength to keep going when I've gone as far as I can.

My beautiful children, De'Asia, Darius and Dayonne who reminds me what love is everyday. They make me feel extremely special how they tell me that they love me and hug every night before they go to bed or before I leave to go anywhere.

I would also like to thank my overseers, Bishop Joseph Ricard, Sr. and Lady Walterine Ricard for allowing me the opportunity to serve, be rebuked and draw from wisdom from them as it relates to serving.

CONTENTS

Introduction

I grew up in church but I started really going to church in 1994 which was the same year I joined the church I am currently attending. Since being here, I have really learned a lot as it relates to ministry as well as ministering in different capacities. Some of which I will be sharing in this book.

The ironic thing is the way this book came about. It started off as a manuscript I felt impressed by the Lord to write concerning serving my pastor. The title of this manuscript is "I Am Some Important Shoes for those Pretty Feet." The scriptural foundation of this title is found in Romans10:15. The title depicts the role servers play in the lives of their leaders. After years of deliberating, proofreading, and having many individuals read over and edit this manuscript, I never moved forward with getting it published as I lacked the inspiration to do so. It was after speaking with my pastor concerning teaching a class on serving that God moved me to turn the manuscript into a book.

This book contains many important key points that are designed to teach individuals how to be, not necessarily armor bearers, but ARM-Bearers that will be able to hold up the hands of their Moses. These lessons came with a price and it is my desire that those who were/are called, chosen and appointed to serve their man and woman of God can apply these lessons and become a great asset to his or her local ministry.

Serving the man and woman of God is a prestigious honor and is not to be taken lightly. Those that are privileged to serve in this capacity have the responsibility of learning multiple things if they desire to be an asset and not a liability to the man and woman of God they serve. Among the many things these servers must learn are the following:

1. <u>KNOW YOUR MINISTRY</u>

> *Romans 12:6-7 Having then gifts differing according to the grace that is given to us, whether prophecy, let us prophesy according to the proportion of faith; 7. Or MINISTRY, let us wait on our ministering: or he that teacheth, on teaching.......*

The word MINISTRY in this portion of scripture in the Greek is "Diakonia" which means by one definition "Service, ministering, especially of those who execute the commands of others", this is also where we get our word Deacon from. King James Dictionary defines a deacon as a server or an attendant. In short, a deacon is a server. These two verses of scripture mention many different positions but ultimately, the word server describes them all. It is important to note that the content of this book is for deacons, executive assistants, adjutants, preachers and etc. There is one primary thing that separates them all and that is The Call. As it is written in 1 Timothy 3:10, deacons, adjutants, security, executive assistants, servers and preachers are to be tested. After they are tested and found acceptable, then they are appointed.

2. <u>KNOW YOUR MISSION</u>

> *1 Chronicles 12:17 And David went out to meet them, and answered and said unto them, If ye be come peaceably unto me to help me, mine heart shall be knit unto you: but if ye be come to betray me to mine enemies, seeing there is no wrong in mine hands, the God of our fathers look thereon, and rebuke it.*
>
> *18 Then the spirit came upon Amasai, who was chief of the captains, and he said, Thine are we, David, and on thy side, thou son of Jesse: peace, peace be unto thee, and peace be to thine helpers; for thy God helpeth thee. Then David received them, and made them captains of the band.*

Here in the 21st Century, many churches have deviated from using the term Armor Bearer and have chosen to allow individuals to serve in other areas under different titles for many different reasons. According to an experienced and seasoned pastor, the loyalty and trustworthiness as in the past and fail meet the criteria to be used as an in that capacity. This is what David wanted to make sure of when they approached him in Ziklag in 1 Chronicles 12. David's first question was to find out their intention. After their answer and period being tested and proven, the bible says that David gave them their mission. He made them captains of the band.

3. <u>KNOW YOUR LEADER</u>

> *John 14:9 Jesus saith unto him, Have I been so long time with you, and yet hast thou not known me, Philip?*

It is possible to be with your leader and still not know him/her. The importance of knowing the heart of your leader is very crucial to being an effective ARM-Bearer.

Furthermore, if you have this workbook or attending this class, then you are one who has either been chosen to serve or acknowledged that this is a position God has charged you to serve in this area of ministry and henceforth the task of increasing in knowledge is now your responsibility. It is my prayer that this information in this workbook will aid and guide you in the direction that will be profitable for you becoming an effective ARM-Bearer.

Many are Called

"How then shall they call on him in whom they have not believed? and how shall they believe in him of whom they have not heard? and how shall they hear without a preacher?

And how shall they preach, except they be sent? as it is written, How beautiful are the feet of them that preach the gospel of peace, and bring glad tidings of good things!"

Romans 10:14-15

A vast amount of people grows up in churches that vary in denominations but can be found to share similar experiences. After attending church for a while, he or she begin to have questions. Some of these individuals' questions are the same and even their reasons for attending church share commonality. These experiences include gradually coming to church, committing to the church by membership and then beginning to work in ministry in departments. Suddenly the questions change. The questions used to be; Is this where I want to join? What can this ministry offer me and my family? Or ultimately, is this where God wants me to be? After committing, now the questions are; What is it that God wants me to do? What is my purpose? Am I walking in my calling?

The moment I was called to a specific duty, a group of other men I and were attending a men's service. I was seated next to my pastor. As I sat there, I found myself looking at his shoes. It felt as funny to me during that time as it sounds to you right now. While looking at my pastor's shoes, the message he preached at a Pastor's Appreciation some years back resurfaced. My pastor preached a message entitled "Man You Have Some Pretty Feet." The scriptures above served as the text. In this message, he elaborated on the importance of pastors and the key roles pastor's play. He stated that the words they preach are echoed from the heart of God to His people. Those words are spirit, life, and are key elements to a life of abundance. This message stayed with me for quite some time. It was not until I had an encounter with God at this men's service, however, that God would speak and say, "I want you to be your pastor's shoes!"

While I did not understand it at first, God went on to explain that in being the shoes of your leaders, you provide three major services. As it is the duty of some, *not all*, to be the preserver of God's man and God's woman whom He has placed over us, SHOES *cover, support, and make them (the leaders) look good.* It is my prayer that as you read and work through this book, this encounter and revelation will help someone that has been called, struggling with the process of the call, or has a heart to preserve their leader.

1. *What area of ministry do you serve in?*

_____

_____

2. *Were you called or chosen to serve in this position? Explain.*

_____

_____

3. *If called, is there a specific duty or area of serving you were called to?*

_____

_____

_____

4. *What do you feel you could do to elevate your level of serving?*

_____

_____

_____

_____

COVER ME UNTIL I RECOVER

And the Lord said, Simon, Simon, behold, Satan hath desired to have you, that He may sift you as wheat:

But I have prayed for thee, that thy faith fail not: and when thou art converted, strengthen thy brethren.

Luke 22:31-32

One can find that there are many different brands, types, and styles of shoe. However, there is one attribute about shoes that many find important. The first attribute is that they <u>cover</u> the feet of an individual.

I heard an individual speak about the thirty-second verse of Luke some time ago. The statement he made was very comical, but it also made sense. He said he could imagine what his own thought process would be if he were the one having that conversation with Jesus instead of Peter. He stated, "After hearing the warning from Jesus, he stated that he would say, *"Lord that's good, and I thank you for your prayer that my faith doesn't fail, but just pray that he don't sift me!"* Once I finished laughing, I began to think, "Yeah, why didn't He pray that Satan not sift him?"

Pastors and first ladies have the daunting task of overseeing many individuals. The responsibilities vary as they have to chart territories that others cannot or would not dare venture into. The road can get rough and tough for them. The Bible says that the steps of a good man are ordered by the Lord, but it does not say that those steps would not have to go over rocky terrain, mountainous areas, and even sometimes wade in deep waters for the sake of rescuing God's beloved. And for the gospel's sake, those beautiful feet are and have been very important in the lives of many people. This is why many cannot afford to allow those chosen by God to watch over God's people, to suffer. It is the responsibility of the chosen vessels of God to *cover* them just as shoes cover the feet.

There are many different ways that a person can cover the man and woman of God. One form is through *continuous prayer*. Just as we sometimes get weary, tired, and feel like giving up; pastors and first ladies are no different. Some expect pastors and first ladies to be superhuman, non-destructive human beings. As leaders over many different size churches, groups of people, and different characters and moods in those churches and groups, it would be safe to say that the responsibility of caring for so many people can be overwhelming at times. Additionally, these same leaders have to also care for their own families and homes. For those who have been blessed to serve in many different areas in ministry, he or she may have seen a situation where the family of his or her pastor and first lady have been put on hold in order to cater to the needs of others in the body of Christ. It is not uncommon for a pastor and first lady who has shown up for scheduled services, conferences, bible studies, preached, taught, and prayed for many in altar calls, to get a call after finally getting home to rest that a loved one is in the hospital. Where many churches have designated people to fulfill these areas of ministry, many individuals desire to see the faces of their leaders. As discomforting as it is to say, I wonder how individuals view their overseers and their expectations of them, but many play the role of Martha in John 11:21 to say "If you and first lady would have been here, my mother, father, sister or brother would not have died, gotten sick, have cancer or even left church. After the leaders have visited, prayed for and comforted individuals, duty calls early the next morning to handle the daily operation and administration of the ministry. In addition to these natural stresses of leading, Satan tries as hard as possible to capitalize on every opportunity to keep our leaders weak. Therefore, it is the *Shoes* responsibility to, as my Bishop would say, "*Cover them until they recover.*"

If I may use the sport of football as an example of the second attribute of the shoe. There are many key people on a football team, however important they are, one of the most important players on the field is the quarterback. It takes a special individual to be a quarterback. They have to be able to see things other players cannot and do not see. They have to be able to read the attacks of their opponents and call plays that will put the team in the best position to score. They have to be able to handle and endure pressure while being attacked from every side and still maintain their composure without giving up. Also, they have to know when to tuck the ball and run. Furthermore, quarterbacks have to be able to block out all noise from the stadium, take time and hear from the coach or play caller in the booth, and communicate the coach's directions accurately. This is why no team is great without an offensive line because the quarterback needs time to make sure he gets the play right and that the play is executed properly.

Once the quarterback has fulfilled his duties, the offensive linemen's job is to protect the quarterback. As the quarterback, this position also requires a special person. The offensive linemen job duties are just as important as the quarterbacks. Furthermore, offensive linemen have to be able to see what other players cannot and do not see, especially what the quarterback does not see. This is not to say that the quarterback cannot see or that the offensive linemen sees more, it's just that most quarterbacks do not try to see everything because they believe and trust the offensive line will *cover* and protect them so they can make an accurate throw. In the Book of Acts chapter 6, there is a depiction of appointing of servers which states; you serve the tables, but while you do this, we will give ourselves continuously to prayer, and to the ministry of the word. In other words, you *cover me* while I continue to feed the wide receivers, tight ends, running backs, full backs, ushers, musicians, laity and body of Christ the football (Word of God). It is in this analogy that we find the importance of staying in position. Opponents search for weaknesses and after it is found, those weaknesses are targeted with the intent of stopping the play as well as taking out the quarterback.

1. *What is your role as a server?*

   _____

   _____

   _____

2. *In the analogy of the football team, what lesson can you learn from this? How would you apply it in your serving?*

   _____

   _____

   _____

3. *How important is it to stay in position? Why is it important?*

   _____

   _____

   _____

4. *Everyone cannot play the same position at the same time and with each position having different duties Identify any other positions or duties that an individual can serve in and duties that can be carried out that are not being done in your local ministry as it relates to serving your leaders?*

   _____

   _____

   _____

   _____

Few Are Chosen

From the illustration of football, it is important to note that offensive linemen are handpicked. Therefore, the responsibility of covering for, blocking for, and protecting the blind side of God's man and God's woman, leaves no room for Judas. A Judas cannot be an offensive lineman.

David's encounter with the Children of Benjamin and Judah paints the picture of the second phase of this revelation of being the important shoes of leaders. The scriptures state:

> *And David went out to meet them, and answered and said unto them, If ye be come peaceably unto me to help me, mine heart shall be knit unto you: but if ye be come to betray me to mine enemies, seeing there is no wrong in mine hands, the God of our fathers look thereon, and rebuke it.*
>
> *Then the spirit came upon Amasai, who was chief of the captains, and he said, Thine are we, David, and on thy side, thou son of Jesse: peace, peace be unto thee, and peace be to thine helpers; for thy God helpeth thee. Then David received them, and made them captains of the band.*
>
> *1 Chronicles 12:17-18*

David gets a visit from the Children of Benjamin seeking to join his band. David, during this time, was reserved about letting anyone in. This is important to note because if we are to be our leader's shoes; many may be called or desire to serve in this capacity, but here is why few are chosen.

It was an honor being called and allowed to be the shoes of my leaders and this book is written for current and aspiring shoes. For those who may read this book but never find themselves in the position to be the shoes of their overseers or leaders; this is not to imply that I was so much better or more qualified than anyone in our church, or in any other church for that matter, but this is to make sure people understand that in order to be the shoes of your leaders, it means getting close. You have to be willing and be allowed by the overseers to get close and everyone cannot handle getting close.

CAN YOU HANDLE "CLOSE"

Getting close is one thing, but what you get close to is what causes the problems. When you are a shoe, you have to endure many things, situations, circumstances, and be placed in places many others cannot handle. Furthermore, you have to be strong enough to make sure that your responsibilities as a shoe are carried out. This is not a position for those who are emotionally unstable or easily offended. The position of being shoes has both negative and positive connotations. It is also unpredictable because one will never know when or for what they are going to be used for.

If we look from a natural standpoint, we buy shoes for many different reasons or occasions. Some of these occasions are work, school, formal, casual, and etc. Whatever the occasion, it is important that the shoe fits properly and are able to handle what they were purchased for. Sometimes shoes are worn for occasions and/or placed in situations they were not purchased for and the shoes provide little or no covering, support, or protection. This is not to say shoes were purchased to be abused, but people buy shoes because: 1. they have the confidence that these are the right shoes for what they need. 2. The shoes are valuable to the individual. 3. They like the shoes or else they wouldn't have purchased them. Also, depending on what kind of shoe was purchased, before being worn, sometimes shoes have to be conditioned. They are put to the test to make sure that the shoe can handle the task of the second attribute of the shoe…. *supporting*.

ARE YOU A GOOD SUPPORTER

Those that came to David to Ziklag stated that *"Thine are we David and we are here to support you!"* *We are on your side.* (1 Chronicles 12)

Shoes are tried on before they are purchased, sometimes; to see how well they fit and the capacity to support the back. In other words, you may be placed or allowed to serve in many different areas of ministry, some of in which you did not seek to serve. You may be called upon to do certain things in and around the ministry during service or by your leaders that may have you questioning why. Though shoes cannot speak, be careful of those single-purpose shoes that may discourage or speak ill of your usage. It is during this time where the statement "many called were not chosen," takes effect. Called or selected shoes are not immediately picked because it is in the preparation (trying on of the shoe) time, your purpose or placement is established.

Many can recall stepping on a nail or a piece of glass and not notice it until you feel something underneath the shoe that we then realize that due to the shoes worn, what could have harmed us did not prevail. I would assume that you were very grateful for those shoes. I would also assume that the lives that were spared because Moses went to God in Exodus 32 were very grateful. So it is with our leaders. If your leaders have been instrumental in any way in preserving or saving your life, or the lives of your loved ones, we too should be very grateful and commit to serving in whatever capacity needed so that the lives of others can be changed.

Exodus 17 shows the importance of support. The Bible records that Israel was in Rephidim and Amalek came out to fight against them. Moses then reaches in his closet and pulls out a pair of shoes and said "Joshua, go out tomorrow and fight against Amalek." The story goes on to say that as Joshua fought in the valley, Moses stood on the cliff and held up his hands. As long as Moses' hands were lifted up, Israel prevailed. When Moses' hands grew weary and began to come down, Amalek prevailed. Here is where the other pair of shoes came in. The Bible says that Aaron and Hur came in and protected and covered Moses' feet……. they stilled his hands. They made sure that Moses had the support needed to endure through the battle until it was won. Nowhere in scripture does it show that Moses had to call for his shoes. In other words, in ministry, many leaders are left uncovered and unsupported because many have witnessed pastors and first ladies doing so much and it is easy to say; "They can handle it." "God has their back and they are strong." In saying those words, individuals rarely see leaders' hands descending and the enemy gaining advantage in the valley. Covering and supporting shoes recognize their leaders growing weary and spring into action. Those that are not chosen are the ones in which Moses had to drop his hands, take his eyes off of Joshua and the other shoes fighting in the valley and go and find shoes that are only used temporarily. Temporary shoes are the walking boots for broken legs that serves a purpose for a season. However important, these conflict with the last duty for a shoe.

To be the shoes for your leaders, one must understand that you serve in one of two categories - Specific-purpose or Multi-purpose. Multi-purpose means that you will be used for whatever situation needed. Specific-purpose, such as a walking boot, means you are rarely used or only used when the purpose has presented itself. Coincidentally, just as the analogy of the football team, both are important simply because one may be called on to serve in either category when needed. This is why getting close is important because the more you are worn the more the wearer gets a feel for how the shoes perform in different situations.

Certain occupations require standing for extending periods of time causing individuals to seek shoes to accommodate this demand. Doctors have recommended orthopedic shoes for those with bad backs so that it will enable the wearer to stand longer and walk further. So it is with leaders. As shoes, their responsibilities are the ability to Support! Leaders seek shoes that will provide the proper support and covering needed to provide them with what they need. To affirm your perseverance, a leader may contact you instantaneously.

To use another illustration, exotic skin shoes, such as crocodiles, have to be handled a certain way. Due to the exotic skin being hard, many people place a hot wet towel across the front of the shoe so that the front of the shoe will soften up. This is so the shoes will not hurt when worn. Sometimes people with wide feet place shoe horns inside their shoes to stretch them out for a proper fit. You might be wondering why I am bringing this up. Simple! You may be serving in your ministry and you are wondering why it seems your leaders are always rebuking you, correcting you, or constantly having you do certain things. Do not fret. You are a multi-purpose shoe and you are just being prepared. After being stretched, bent, and placed under a hot wet towel, when it is time for you to be released to lead, you will have already gone through your time of preparation.

During preparation, you will endure the sweat of your leader as a shoe. You will endure the movements of your leaders as a shoe (going where he/she goes). You will be exposed to some of the stumbles and slips, of which many people cannot handle, of your leaders as a shoe. You will even be stored away sometimes in the closet or private places where many others cannot go as a shoe. You will get to know the character of your leader rather than the position of your leader as a shoe. As a result of the closeness and privileges shoes are exposed to, the shoes have to be able to do what the Children of Benjamin assured David they came to do........ HAVE THEIR BACK! Once again, I reiterate, JUDAS' CANNOT BE SHOES!

EVALUATE

Take this time to rate yourself as a *SHOE by placing the number 1, 2, or 3 next to each of the following statements:*

1. YES   2. NO   3. SOMETIMES

	I fully understand my role as a shoe.
	With my understanding of my role, I am excited and take pride in serving to the fullest of my abilities.
	I can recognize what my leader needs before he/she asks and seek to accommodate before being asked.
	I do not believe I am in the right position.
	I can recognize the state my leaders are in emotionally, physically, and spiritually and are affected by it.
	I have and keep a good line of communication with my leaders.
	I can handle being corrected.
	I am comfortable with that tasks I am given as a shoe.
	If I am not comfortable with the given tasks, I communicate it to my leaders immediately.
	I know what my leaders expect of me.
	If I am not clear of my expectations, I communicate it to my leaders immediately.
	I am comfortable being challenged to grow as a shoe.
	I am very timid/shy when it comes to serving.
	I know the importance of availing myself to my leaders and do so to the best of my ability.
	It hurts when I am not acknowledged for the

	work I have done for my leaders.
	TOTAL
31-45	I understand my role as a shoe and know what kind of shoe I am. (Permanent/Temporary/NO)
16–30	I am a temporary shoe but I now understand my worth and seek to grown in my role to become a better shoe. (Permanent)
1-15	I am a walking boot/shoe and do not have the desire to expand. I am satisfied where I am.
Questions may vary based on the structure of the ministry/church. This can be modified.	

SERVE THE SERVER

For a period of time, while I was in preparation, God had me doing certain things. My pastor had an armor bearer and a server at this particular time and I used to watch how they served and took care of certain tasks for him. This allowed him more time to take care of more pressing issues that needed attention. God impressed in my heart to do something that later blessed me tremendously. He told me to *serve the servers*. God instructed me to buy breakfast items, drinks, and even run errands that were generally done by my pastor's armor bearer and server. I would only seek to do those tasks that would be allowed by my pastor because at this time I did not know his heartbeat, movements, mannerisms, and simply put, I was not an established shoe yet. This allowed the armor bearer and server to be more available for my pastor, and the more they were available the more important tasks they could do. The more they could do for my pastor, the more my pastor could be God-ward for the people.

Exodus 18:14 And when Moses' father-in-law saw all that he did to the people, he said, What is this thing that thou doest to the people? why sittest thou thyself alone, and all the people stand by thee from morning unto even?

15 And Moses said unto his father-in-law, Because the people come unto me to enquire of God:

16 When they have a matter, they come unto me; and I judge between one and another, and I do make them know the statutes of God, and his laws.

17 And Moses' father-in-law said unto him, the thing that thou doest is not good.

18 Thou wilt surely wear away, both thou, and this people that is with thee: for this thing is too heavy for thee; thou art not able to perform it thyself alone.

19 Hearken now unto my voice, I will give thee counsel, and God shall be with thee: Be thou for the people to God-ward, that thou mayest bring the causes unto God:

20 And thou shalt teach them ordinances and laws, and shalt shew them the way wherein they must walk, and the work that they must do.

21 Moreover thou shalt provide out of all the people able men, such as fear God, men of truth, hating covetousness; and place such over them, to be rulers of thousands, and rulers of hundreds, rulers of fifties, and rulers of tens:

22 And let them judge the people at all seasons: and it shall be, that every great matter they shall bring unto thee, but every small matter they shall judge: so shall it be easier for thyself, and they shall bear the burden with thee.

23 If thou shalt do this thing, and God command thee so, then thou shalt be able to endure, and all this people shall also go to their place in peace.

The above scriptures found in Exodus 18 shows Jethro's concern for Moses because of the responsibilities Moses had and is the testimony of many that love their David, Moses, Pastor, etc., and it should be the concern as shoes that they do not wear away.

1. *How well do you know your leaders?*

_____

_____

2. *How much time do you spend learning them?*

_____

_____

3. *How important do you think this attribute is? Why?*

_____

_____

4. *How often do you place yourself in a position to learn or be used by your leaders?*

_____

_____

5. *What have you done thus far to learn or be used by your leaders?* _____

_____

_____

Note: It is important in your journey to learn your leaders and be able to serve him/her and beware of your company and surroundings.

A Compliment Goes a Long Way

*Let your light so shine before men, that
they may see your good works and glorify your
Father which is in heaven.*

Matthew 5:16

In my spiritual journey of over 20 years, I have witnessed several things such as people entering and exiting the ministry and the glory of God filling the house to a point where His presence is undeniable, where no one can doubt or error in the realization that......Truly God was and still dwell in the temple!!! The concept of being the shoes of your leader is not seen in how a service went. It's not seen in how well one shouts, sings, or even preaches or how well the man and woman of God preaches, how many lives were touched and changed, due to wearing the right shoes. This means that if the first two steps were carried out properly, the man and/or woman of God had plenty of time to get in the presence of God to hear from Him and prepare to embrace the platform and minister to God's people. The "behind the scenes" is where the shoes are most important.

Many churches are organized like businesses, and like businesses, many people/servers have left because they felt as if they were unappreciated or not complimented. I recently heard Bishop T. D. Jakes say that he posed a question on twitter that asked "What do you expect from your church?" He went on to say that he received a large number of responses from many of his followers. After receiving that large number of responses, he went on to post another question that says; "What can your church expect from you?" This question yielded minimal amounts of responses. God has anointed and gifted many to serve and not to be served, because God is not unfair, He says in His word that your gift will make room for you and set you before great men. It also says that every good and perfect gift comes from above. To accompany that, He says that He is not unrighteous to forget your work and labor of love. So if I were to interpret this, I would say that God provided the gift, the job, and the reward himself and chose you to operate in whatever capacity he has allowed you to serve in. I also believe that God will reward.

The dictionary defines complement in two forms, as a noun and as a verb. As a noun, complement means "a thing that completes or brings to perfection." As a verb, complement means "Add to (something) in a way that enhances or improves it; make perfect." As shoes, God revealed to me that come what may, I am to Make My Leaders Look Good!

I WAS SHAPED FOR THIS

This role takes major commitment, gets little or no recognition at times, and produces some of the best leaders. After going through the shaping process, shoes are picked to be key leaders over different ministries or perform different tasks. Shoes are called upon to do what many, even the shoes themselves, feel they don't qualify for.

It is my assumption that Moses had plenty of people that could fight. However, when the time came to fight, Moses went into his closet and said, "Joshua, go and get some more shoes and go down tomorrow and fight with Amalek." Joshua did not tell Moses that he had to check his schedule or bring up his own agenda, neither did he ask or state, "Why aren't you going up there? You can fight too!" As a result of Joshua's attitude, as a shoe, an important factor, God says, "Joshua, my servant Moses is dead," which you know the rest of that story.

Shoes receive many rebukes, corrections, bumps, bruises, and even seemed to be overlooked, but it is the shoes that are chosen to represent or complement the leaders in prestigious situations. This is true because shoes get broken in. Shoes, regardless of how they look, are rarely thrown away because over time, the shoes have been formed and fashioned to fit its wearer. If the wearer has flat feet or bowed legs to where the foot leans to the side, you will often find people who have shoes on to where the heel has been worn so much until it leans with the foot. This is called having the heartbeat of your leader. These are those who have stood the test of time, endured the bumps, bruises, sweat, tears, late night pacing, bending at the toe from long nights of praying, and have proven to be very valuable and reliable to be a Coverer, Supporter, and make the leaders look Good.

It Is What It Is

If I then, your Lord and Master, have washed your feet; ye also ought to wash one another's feet.

For I have given you an example, that ye should do as I have done to you.

Verily, verily, I say unto you, The servant is not greater than his lord; neither he that is sent greater than he that sent him.

If ye know these things, happy are ye if ye do them.

I speak not of you all: I know whom I have chosen: but that the scripture may be fulfilled, He that eateth bread with me hath lifted up his heel against me.

John 13:14-18

18. I am not referring to all of you; I know those I have chosen. But this is to fulfill this passage of Scripture: 'He who shared my bread has turned[a] against me.' (NIV)

Just in case you missed the theme of this workbook and you are still wondering what in the world shoes are, shoes are servers. It is what it is!

This workbook is written for those who are called and will commit to serving in a high position without seeking a high position to serve in. This is also to serve notice that shoes do not serve for notoriety or public status, but because our Lord Jesus Christ did it. So for those who have walked away from being shoes because people called you a flunky, brown nose, or yes man, return to your work. As the scripture says, everyone can't do this job. Jesus even said in verse 18 of the NIV *"I am not referring to all of you; I know those I have chosen."* You have been chosen for this and have been anointed to serve your leaders.

Jesus sets the precedent when He says "I came not to be ministered unto, but to minister" and "If your Lord and Master have washed your feet, ye also ought to wash one another's feet. For I have given you an example that ye should do as I have done to you....... SERVE!

Serving the Lord, as well as your leaders, pays off. Don't despise God's calling and your opportunity to be the shoes of your leaders because you are some important shoes for those pretty feet.

www.ingramcontent.com/pod-product-compliance
Lightning Source LLC
Chambersburg PA
CBHW071449040426
42445CB00012BA/1495